ARGENTINA 2016 HUMAN RIGHTS REPORT

Note: This report was updated 4/26/17; see Appendix F: Errata for more information.

EXECUTIVE SUMMARY

Argentina is a federal constitutional republic. In November 2015 Mauricio Macri won election to the presidency in the second round of multiparty elections that the media and various nongovernmental organizations (NGOs) described as generally free and fair. The 2015 first round also included legislative elections for one-half of the Chamber of Deputies and one-third of the Senate.

Civilian authorities maintained effective control over the security forces.

The principal human rights problems included multiple reports of official corruption, torture by federal and provincial police, and gender-based violence.

Other human rights problems included use of excessive force by police, harsh prison conditions, arbitrary arrest and detention, prolonged pretrial detention, judicial inefficiency, child abuse, anti-Semitism, discrimination against and infringements on the rights of indigenous people, sex trafficking, forced labor, and child labor.

Judicial authorities indicted and prosecuted a number of current and former government officials who committed abuses during the year, including a number of investigations against high-level officials of the former government.

Section 1. Respect for the Integrity of the Person, Including Freedom from:

a. Arbitrary Deprivation of Life and other Unlawful or Politically Motivated Killings

There was no information available during the year regarding arbitrary or unlawful killings by police.

The Center for Legal and Social Studies (CELS) reported 126 deaths during 2015 as a result of police using unwarranted or excessive force in the metropolitan area of Buenos Aires.

In February authorities elevated to a criminal cause of action the April 2015 killing of a youth in San Martin, Buenos Aires Province, by a police officer on patrol. The officer chased two youths who were suspected of stealing a motorcycle and shot at them as they fled on the motorcycle, killing the passenger. Following the incident authorities dismissed the officer for excessive use of force.

b. Disappearance

There were no reports of politically motivated disappearances.

Authorities continued to investigate and prosecute individuals implicated in disappearances, killings, and torture committed during the 1976-83 military dictatorship. On August 25, the Cordoba Federal Oral Courthouse No. 1 sentenced former Third Army Corps commander Luciano Benjamin Menendez to an additional life term in prison for murder, torture, and crimes against humanity, bringing his full sentence to 14 prison terms and 12 consecutive life sentences for human rights violations. Menendez was one of 43 defendants in the La Perla megatrial. Six defendants were acquitted, while the others received sentences ranging from two years to life imprisonment. On March 29, the Salta Federal Oral Court convicted former bus company owner Marcos Levin for conspiring with two former police officers to kidnap and torture a former employee in 1977. The court sentenced Levin to 12 years in prison, making him the first businessman to be sentenced for crimes against humanity during the military dictatorship era.

Judicial authorities continued to investigate cases of kidnapping and illegal adoption of children born to detained dissidents by members of the former military dictatorship. On October 4, the NGO Abuelas de la Plaza de Mayo reported that the 121st missing grandchild of the estimated 500 persons born to detained and missing dissidents during the dictatorship and illegally adopted by former military officials had been identified and made aware of his background.

The Argentine Forensic Anthropology Team continued cooperation with the National Institute of Industrial Technology, which provides technical support and assistance in the identification of remains of victims of the military junta.

c. Torture and Other Cruel, Inhuman, or Degrading Treatment or Punishment

The law prohibits torture and other cruel, inhuman, or degrading treatment or punishment and provides penalties for torture similar to those for homicide.

NGOs, CELS, the Prosecutor General's Office, the Penitentiary Authority (an independent government body that monitors prison conditions), and the Buenos Aires Provincial Memory Commission's Committee against Torture (an autonomous office established by the provincial government) reported complaints of torture perpetrated by provincial and federal prison officials.

No unified registration system to record acts and victims of torture exists at the federal level.

The Buenos Aires Provincial Criminal Court of Cassation's Office of Public Defenders reported that from January to April there were 221 complaints of torture and mistreatment by law enforcement officers during arrest or institutional confinement, of which 52 cases involved minors. A 2015 Santa Fe Provincial Office of Public Defenders survey, the latest available information, reported 503 alleged victims of abuse, mistreatment, and human rights violations committed by provincial security force personnel in the penitentiary system. According to the report, 21 percent of the victims were 18 years old or younger, and mistreatment most frequently occurred in detention centers and while in transit.

On July 18, a court sentenced five police officers from the Buenos Aires Provincial Police to life imprisonment for the torture and murder of detainee Gaston Duffau in the locality of Ramos Mejia in 2008.

Prison and Detention Center Conditions

Prison conditions often were harsh due to overcrowding, poor medical care, and unsanitary conditions. Particularly in the province of Buenos Aires, there were reports of forced transfers and the recurrent use of solitary confinement as a method of punishment.

Physical Conditions: While prison capacity in federal penitentiaries was marginally adequate (approximately 103 percent of capacity), prisoners in Buenos Aires provincial penitentiaries exceeded facility capacity by an estimated 87 percent, according to a CELS report during the year. Many pretrial detainees were held with convicted prisoners.

Inmates in many facilities suffered from overcrowding; poor nutrition; inadequate medical and psychological treatment; inadequate sanitation, heating, ventilation, and light; limited family visits; and frequent degrading treatment, according to reports by human rights organizations and research centers.

Overcrowding in juvenile facilities often resulted in minors being held in police station facilities, although some NGOs and the national prison ombudsman noted the law prohibited doing so.

Women's prisons were generally less violent, dangerous, and crowded than men's prisons. Pregnant prisoners were exempted from work and rigorous physical exercise and were transferred to the penitentiary clinic prior to their delivery date. Children born to women in prison may remain in a special area of the prison with the mother until the age of four and receive daycare.

According to the Penitentiary Prosecutors Office of the Nation, 257 cases of torture and mistreatment were registered in the Federal Penitentiary Service during the first semester of the year; however, only 42 percent of the complaints of torture and bad treatment resulted in criminal investigations.

The Federal Penitentiary Service reported 20 inmate deaths in federal prisons, seven of which were violent, between January and June; however, CELS statistics for the province of Buenos Aires for 2015 reflected 50 prisoners died from violence, while another 89 died from health problems and lack of medical attention.

<u>Administration</u>: Information on the adequacy of recordkeeping was unavailable. Authorities permitted prisoners and detainees to submit complaints to judicial authorities without censorship and to request investigation of credible allegations of inhuman conditions. Local NGOs noted, however, that access to a public defender was sometimes limited and that prisoners occasionally did not submit complaints to authorities due to fear of reprisal.

<u>Independent Monitoring</u>: The government usually permitted monitoring by independent local and international human rights observers.

d. Arbitrary Arrest or Detention

The law prohibits arbitrary arrest and detention, and the government generally observed these prohibitions.

On October 21, the UN Working Group on Arbitrary Detention called for the release of Tupac Amaru social activist Milagro Sala, opining that her preventive detention was arbitrary. On January 16, authorities arrested Sala as she led a protest against the Jujuy provincial government's reforms to social spending. Authorities initially charged Sala with sedition; however, the Jujuy province prosecutor later dropped the sedition count and brought new charges of assault, fraud, and embezzlement of public funds. International NGOs criticized the detention and the provincial government's rejection of the UN Working Group's opinion. On December 28, a federal court convicted Sala of "aggravated material damages" and sentenced her to a three-year suspended prison sentence. On December 29, Sala was convicted by a state court of civil disturbances charges. She was fined 4,363 pesos ($235) and prohibited from holding office in any civil organization.

Role of the Police and Security Apparatus

The federal police generally have jurisdiction for maintaining law and order in the federal capital and for federal crimes in the provinces. Other federal police authorities include the airport security police, the Gendarmerie, the Coast Guard, and the Bureau of Prisons. All federal police forces fall under the authority of the Ministry of Security. Each province, including the city of Buenos Aires, also has its own police force that responds to a provincial (or municipal) security ministry or secretariat. Individual forces varied considerably in their effectiveness and respect for human rights. The armed forces fall under the Ministry of Defense and by law do not participate in internal security. Through executive decree the government sought to expand the scope of the armed forces to provide logistics support and surveillance of national borders. The federal security forces have authority to conduct internal investigations into alleged abuses and to dismiss individuals who allegedly committed a human rights violation. In September the minister of security dispatched additional federal security force personnel to Santa Fe Province for one year to combat complex crime and corruption.

The federal government can file complaints about alleged abuses with the federal courts, and provincial governments can do the same for provincial security forces. Members of security forces convicted of a crime were subject to stiff penalties. Authorities generally administratively suspended officers accused of wrongdoing until their investigations were completed. Authorities investigated and in some cases detained, prosecuted, and convicted the officers involved; however, impunity at the federal and provincial level remained a problem.

Arrest Procedures and Treatment of Detainees

Police generally apprehended individuals openly with warrants based on sufficient evidence and issued by a duly authorized official. Police may detain suspects for up to 10 hours without an arrest warrant if authorities have a well-founded belief they have committed or are about to commit a crime or police are unable to determine the suspect's identity. Human rights groups reported that police occasionally arrested persons arbitrarily and detained suspects longer than 10 hours.

The law provides detainees with the right to a prompt determination of the legality of their detention by a lower criminal court judge, who determines whether to proceed with an investigation. In some cases there were delays in this process and in informing detainees of the charges against them.

The law provides for the right to bail except in cases involving flight risk or risk of subornation of justice.

Authorities allowed detainees prompt access to counsel and provided public defenders if they were unable to afford counsel. In some cases such access was delayed due to an overburdened system.

Arbitrary Arrest: Police on occasion arrested and detained citizens arbitrarily.

Pretrial Detention: The law provides for investigative detention of up to two years for indicted persons awaiting or undergoing trial; the period may be extended by one year in limited circumstances. The slow pace of the justice system often resulted in lengthy detentions beyond the period stipulated by law. A June census carried out by the Federal Penitentiary Service revealed that in Buenos Aires Province prisons, 61 percent of prisoners were either in pretrial confinement or awaiting a final sentence. According to several human rights organizations, 30 percent of pretrial detainees were eventually acquitted. A convicted prisoner usually receives credit for time served.

Detainee's Ability to Challenge Lawfulness of Detention before a Court: Persons arrested or detained, regardless of whether on criminal or other grounds, are entitled to challenge in court the legal basis or arbitrary nature of their detention and obtain prompt release and compensation if found to have been unlawfully detained.

e. Denial of Fair Public Trial

While the constitution and law provide for an independent judiciary, the government did not always respect judicial independence. According to local NGOs, judges in some federal criminal and ordinary courts were subject at times to political manipulation. NGOs also criticized all three branches of the government for use of inappropriate procedures for selecting judges and for manipulating the assignment of judges to specific cases.

A law enacted in June 2015 allowed the Magistrates' Council to designate "substitute judges" from congressionally approved lists of judges, attorneys, and court secretaries, circumventing the normal qualifying and order of merit criteria reserved for permanent appointments. Media reported that the government selected substitute judges sympathetic to its interests. In November 2015 the Supreme Court ruled the law providing for the appointment of substitute judges was unconstitutional. Nonetheless, the civil society organization Fores reported that almost 25 percent of judges remained "substitute" or temporary judges.

Trial Procedures

The law provides for the right to a fair trial, and an independent judiciary generally enforced this right.

Trials are generally public. In federal and provincial courts, all defendants enjoy a presumption of innocence and have the right to legal counsel and free interpretation from the moment charged through all appeals, to remain silent, to call defense witnesses, and to appeal. If needed, a public defender is provided at public expense when defendants face serious criminal charges. During the investigative stage, defendants can submit questions in writing. A panel of judges decides guilt or innocence. Although defendants and their attorneys have access to government-held evidence, local NGOs indicated defendants sometimes experienced obstacles or delays in obtaining such evidence. Defendants can present witnesses and provide expert witness reports, in addition to the defendant's own evidence. Defendants have the right to be present at their hearings, and there is no trial in absentia. The law extends the above rights to all defendants.

Lengthy delays, procedural logjams, long gaps in the appointment of permanent judges, inadequate administrative support, and general inefficiency hampered the judicial system. Judges' broad discretion on whether and how to pursue investigations contributed to a public perception that many decisions were arbitrary.

Federal and provincial courts continued the transition to trials with oral arguments in criminal cases, replacing the old system of written submissions. Cordoba, Neuquen, Chaco, and Buenos Aires provinces provide defendants accused of certain serious crimes the right to a trial by jury. Additionally, Chaco and Neuquen provinces approved legislation in September 2015 to include special provisions establishing a reserved quota for women and indigenous representatives.

In 2014 Congress enacted supplementary legislation implementing a new criminal procedure code, but the government delayed full implementation until 2017. The law transforms the country's hybrid federal inquisitive system into a full accusatory system, with expanded prosecution under the authority of the attorney general and trial by jury. The new criminal code imposes time limitations on prosecutions (most cases under the new system must be disposed of in three years), expands victims' rights, and provides for expedited deportations of foreigners in lieu of prosecution. The code also creates direct interaction between security forces and prosecutors, who will assume prosecutorial responsibilities currently exercised by investigating magistrates.

Political Prisoners and Detainees

There were no reports of political prisoners or detainees.

Civil Judicial Procedures and Remedies

Citizens have access to the courts to bring lawsuits seeking damages or the protection of rights provided by the constitution.

f. Arbitrary or Unlawful Interference with Privacy, Family, Home, or Correspondence

The constitution prohibits such actions, and the government generally respected these prohibitions. On July 25, the National Administration for Social Security (ANSES) and the Secretariat of Public Communications under the Chief of Staff's Office officially announced an interagency information-sharing agreement. The agreement would make the ANSES database of citizen personal information available to facilitate government public-service communications to the population. A group of citizens, including some opposition legislators, filed a criminal complaint alleging the practice constituted a violation of the right to privacy. On September 7, a lower federal court dismissed the charge, stating the facts alleged failed to constitute a crime. On September 8, a prosecutor appealed the decision, and at year's end the case remained on appeal.

Section 2. Respect for Civil Liberties, Including:

a. Freedom of Speech and Press

The constitution provides for freedom of speech and press, and the government generally respected these rights. Independent newspapers, radio and television outlets, and internet sites were numerous and active, expressing a wide variety of views.

Press and Media Freedoms: On August 24, the government issued a resolution limiting the use of advertising funds for political purposes and established criteria in line with inter-American standards. Thereafter, some newspapers, magazines, and websites that benefited from the distribution of public advertising money during the former administration--which multiple observers asserted was unbalanced and discriminatory in favor of media sources that supported government policies--either shut down or faced serious economic problems.

Violence and Harassment: There were reports of physical attacks, threats, and harassment against journalists in relation to their reporting, most of which covered cases of official corruption.

On April 11, unknown assailants attacked a journalist from television Channel TN who was covering former president Cristina Kirchner's departure from Santa Cruz. The following day assailants attacked Radio Mitre reporters while they reported Kirchner's appearance in court in Buenos Aires.

On September 4, an anonymous individual threatened well-known journalist Luis Majul via text message while he was interviewing a protected witness in a legal case involving former administration officials.

Two armed assailants who broke into the home of radio journalist Sergio Hurgado in December 2015 remained in pretrial detention while their criminal prosecution continued. Hurtado regularly reported on drug use and trafficking in San Antonio Areco, Buenos Aires Province. The assailants, known to local residents for selling drugs, issued Hurtado a warning: "Stop talking about drugs on the radio. We had orders to kill you." Both assailants raped Hurtado's wife, with the journalist's children sleeping nearby, before stealing money and property.

<u>Censorship or Content Restrictions</u>: On March 20, Roberto Navarro of television station C5N alleged that his program *Politica Economica* was cancelled for one day for "political reasons." Navarro said that he planned to broadcast a special report portraying a business partner of President Mauricio Macri in a negative light.

<u>Actions to Expand Press Freedom</u>: On April 6, Congress eliminated the former Audiovisual Communications Enforcement Authority and another media oversight agency and created a single National Communications Authority. President Macri introduced the changes to the Audiovisual Communications Services Act by way of an executive decree in December 2015.

On September 29, the government established a protocol to protect journalists in cases where their activities entail risks, allowing journalists to request protective measures from the Ministry of Security. Measures include confidentiality of the subject matter, nature, scope, and details of the research as well as the protection of personal data of the journalists or third parties related to the investigation.

Internet Freedom

The government did not restrict or disrupt access to the internet or censor online content, and there were no credible reports that the government monitored private online communications without appropriate legal authority. Individuals and groups could engage in the expression of views via the internet, including the use of e-mail and social networks. The World Bank reported that 69 percent of citizens used the internet in 2015.

Academic Freedom and Cultural Events

There were no government restrictions on academic freedom or cultural events.

b. Freedom of Peaceful Assembly and Association

The constitution provides for the freedoms of assembly and association, and the government generally respected these rights.

c. Freedom of Religion

See the Department of State's *International Religious Freedom Report* at
www.state.gov/religiousfreedomreport/.

d. Freedom of Movement, Internally Displaced Persons, Protection of Refugees, and Stateless Persons

The constitution provides for freedom of internal movement, foreign travel,
emigration, and repatriation, and the government generally respected these rights.

The government cooperated with the Office of the UN High Commissioner for
Refugees and other humanitarian organizations in providing protection and
assistance to refugees, asylum seekers, and other persons of concern.

Protection of Refugees

Access to Asylum: The law provides for the granting of refugee status, and the
government has established a system for providing protection to refugees.
Decisions on asylum petitions may take up to two years to adjudicate.

Section 3. Freedom to Participate in the Political Process

The constitution provides citizens the ability to choose their government in free
and fair periodic elections held by secret ballot and based on universal and equal
suffrage.

Elections and Political Participation

Recent Elections: The country held a first round of presidential and legislative
elections in October 2015 and conducted the run-off election for the presidency in
November 2015. Voters elected more than one-half of the members of the
Chamber of Deputies, representing all of the provinces and the city of Buenos
Aires, and one-third of the members of the Senate, representing eight provinces. In
22 of the 24 provinces, citizens elected new governors. Local and international
observers considered the elections generally free and fair.

Participation of Women and Minorities: No laws limit participation of women and
minorities in the political process, and they did participate. Three of 22 cabinet
ministers were women; 38.5 percent of Deputies and 41.7 percent of Senators in
the National Congress were women. The composition of women legislators in the
country's 24 provinces ranged from a low of 20 percent in Santa Fe to a high of 47

percent in Tierra del Fuego. On October 3, the province of Buenos Aires enacted the Gender Parity Law, which requires that any electoral list of candidates for Buenos Aires provincial and municipal bodies must contain equal percentages of male and female gender candidates. The law states that gender is determined by the national identity document, in which a person may register gender of preference regardless of their biological sex. It also states that in the case of resignation, leave of office, or death of elected official, the replacement must be the same gender.

Section 4. Corruption and Lack of Transparency in Government

The law provides criminal penalties for corruption by officials; nonetheless, multiple reports alleged that executive, legislative, and judicial officials engaged in corrupt practices with impunity, suggesting a failure to implement the law effectively. Weak institutions and an often ineffective and politicized judicial system undermined systematic attempts to curb corruption.

Corruption: Cases of corruption occurred in some security forces. The most frequent abuses included extortion of, and protection for, those involved in drug trafficking, human trafficking, money laundering, and the promotion of prostitution.

On June 30, a federal judge indicted former Kirchner administration secretary for public works Jose Lopez for corruption and unjust enrichment. Police observed and videotaped Lopez hiding approximately nine million dollars in cash and luxury watches inside a remote convent in Buenos Aires Province. During the year the Office of Anti-Corruption participated in the prosecution and reviewed infrastructure contracts Lopez supervised while in office 2002-15.

Allegations of corruption in provincial as well as in federal courts remained frequent. A trial date remained pending for former vice president Amado Boudou, who was indicted in 2014 for illicit enrichment and other lesser offenses.

Financial Disclosure: Public officials are subject to financial disclosure laws, and the Ministry of Justice and Human Rights' Anti-Corruption Office is responsible for analyzing and investigating federal executive branch officials, based on their financial disclosure forms. The law provides for public disclosure, but not all agencies complied, and enforcement remained a problem. The Anti-Corruption Office is also responsible for investigating corruption within the federal executive branch and in matters involving federal funds, except for funds transferred to the provinces. As part of the executive branch, the office does not have authority to prosecute cases independently, but it can refer cases to other agencies or serve as the plaintiff and request a judge to initiate a case. The Anti-Corruption Office analyzed 243 cases of noncompliance during the first half of the year. The office referred 25 cases for legal proceedings and dismissed 169 cases. During the same period, the office initiated 109 administrative investigations against government employees for noncompliance with the financial disclosure requirement and referred one case to the court for alleged illicit enrichment.

Public Access to Information: On September 14, Congress passed a law on public access to information. The law explicitly applies to all three branches of the federal government, the public justice offices, and entities such as businesses, political parties, universities, and trade associations that receive public funding. Responses to citizen requests for public information must be answered within 15 days, with an additional 15-day extension available for "exceptional" circumstances. Sanctions apply for noncompliance. The law exempts classified information for defense or foreign policy reasons, as well as information that could endanger the functioning of the financial system, trade secrets, or in commercial, financial, and scientific cases where disclosure could adversely affect competition. The law also mandates the creation of the Agency for Access to Public Information, an autonomous office within the executive branch.

Section 5. Governmental Attitude Regarding International and Nongovernmental Investigation of Alleged Violations of Human Rights

A wide variety of domestic and international human rights groups generally operated without government restriction, investigating and publishing their findings on human rights cases. Government officials usually were cooperative and generally responsive to their views.

Government Human Rights Bodies: The government has a human rights secretariat within the Ministry of Justice and Human Rights. Its main objective is to coordinate within the ministry and collaborate with other ministries and the judiciary to promote policies, plans, and programs for the protection of human rights. During the year it published leaflets and books on a range of human rights topics.

The prosecutor general's Office of Crimes against Humanity investigated and documented human rights violations that occurred under the 1976-83 military dictatorship.

Section 6. Discrimination, Societal Abuses, and Trafficking in Persons

Women

Rape and Domestic Violence: Rape, including spousal rape, is a crime, but evidentiary requirements, either in the form of clear physical injury or in the testimony of a witness, often presented difficulties in prosecuting such crimes. The penalties for rape range from six months' to 20 years' imprisonment. There were no reports of police or judicial reluctance to act on rape cases; women's rights advocates, however, claimed that the attitudes of police, hospitals, and courts toward survivors of sexual violence sometimes revictimized them. They noted a lack of interest in or training for law enforcement officials in protecting survivors or enforcing measures against aggressors, a lack of gender training for legal aid lawyers, and judicial responses that were insufficient to stop domestic violence.

An April report by the Secretariat of Criminal Policy, Ministry of Security, reported that during 2015, there were 3,484 prosecutions for rape, representing an incidence of 8.7 victims per 100,000 inhabitants. Many rapes went unreported due to fear of further violence, retribution, and social stigma.

The law prohibits domestic violence, including spousal abuse, which is broadly defined by a 2009 federal statute to include physical, psychological, and economic violence. Survivors of domestic violence may secure protective measures through the civil courts. Family court judges have the right to bar a perpetrator from a victim's home or workplace. The law requires the state to open a criminal investigation, potentially resulting in life imprisonment, in cases where violence results in death. The law imposes stricter penalties on those who kill their spouses, partners, or children as a consequence of their gender. According to local NGOs, lack of police and judicial vigilance often led to a lack of protection for victims.

On July 29, a Buenos Aires City Court of Appeals ordered a person accused of committing domestic violence and his alleged victim to wear geolocation devices in order for authorities to monitor compliance with a restraining order issued in the case.

The National Register of Femicides, maintained by the Supreme Court Women's Office, recorded that 235 women died as a result of domestic or gender-based violence during 2015. In 20 percent of the cases, the victim had applied for a restraining order or had previously filed a complaint against the male perpetrator.

More than 70 percent of the killings involved a husband, boyfriend, or former boyfriend.

The Supreme Court's Office of Domestic Violence provided around-the-clock protection and resources to victims of domestic violence. The office received approximately 805 cases of domestic violence in the city of Buenos Aires during the first nine months of the year, approximately 62 percent of which involved violence against women. The office also carried out risk assessments necessary to obtain a restraining order.

Public and private institutions offered prevention programs and provided support and treatment for abused women. The Buenos Aires Municipal Government operated a small shelter for battered women.

On July 26, the government published the first national action plan to reduce violence against women, which was scheduled to go into effect in 2017. The plan increases spending on women's rights initiatives, public awareness campaigns to combat sexual and gender-based violence, and innovative technologies to help victims receive treatment and protection.

Sexual Harassment: The law prohibits sexual harassment in the public sector and imposes disciplinary or corrective measures. In some jurisdictions, such as the city of Buenos Aires, sexual harassment might lead to the abuser's dismissal, whereas in others, such as Santa Fe Province, the maximum penalty is five days in prison.

Reproductive Rights: Couples and individuals generally have the right to decide the number, spacing, and timing of their children; manage their reproductive health; and have access to the information and means to do so, free from discrimination, coercion, and violence.

Civil society groups asserted that a 2012 Supreme Court ruling reaffirming a woman's right to terminate pregnancy in all circumstances permitted by law, including as a result of rape, irrespective of the woman's intellectual or psychosocial capacity, was not uniformly applied.

On August 18, authorities provisionally released "Belen," the pseudonym for a 27-year-old woman from the province of Tucuman, from prison. On April 16, a provincial court sentenced Belen to eight years in prison for aggravated homicide; Tucuman authorities had claimed her 2014 miscarriage was an induced abortion. The provincial court freed her after national and international human rights groups protested her imprisonment and the Ministry of Justice and Human Rights filed a motion of concern over irregularities in her case. At year's end Belen remained free on appeal of her conviction.

Discrimination: Although women enjoyed the same legal status and rights as men, they continued to face economic discrimination and held a disproportionately high number of lower-paying jobs. Women also held significantly fewer executive positions in the private sector than men, according to several studies. Although equal payment for equal work is constitutionally mandated, women earned approximately 27 percent less than men earned for similar or equal work.

The Supreme Court's Office of Women trained judges, secretaries, and clerks to handle court cases related to women's issues and ensure equal access for women to positions in the court system. The office also trained judges, prosecutors, judicial staff, and law enforcement agents to increase awareness of gender-related crimes and develop techniques to address gender-related cases and victims.

Children

Birth Registration: The government provides universal birth registration, and citizenship is derived both by birth within the country's territory and from one's parents. Parents have 40 days to register births, and the state has an additional 20 days to do so. The Ministry of Interior and Transportation may issue birth certificates to children under the age of 12 whose births were not previously registered.

Child Abuse: Child abuse was common; the Supreme Court's Office of Domestic Violence reported that 30 percent of the complaints it received involved children. On November 19, in partnership with the UN Children's Fund, the government started the first national campaign against child abuse. In addition to a publicity campaign on television and radio to raise awareness for the incidence of child sexual abuse and mistreatment of children, the government launched a 24/7 hotline staffed by professional child psychologists for free consultations and advice.

Early and Forced Marriage: The legal minimum age of marriage for men and women is 18.

Sexual Exploitation of Children: Sexual exploitation of children, including in prostitution, was a problem. The minimum age of consensual sex is 13, but there are heightened protections for persons ages 13 to 16. There is a statutory rape law with penalties ranging from six months to 20 years in prison, depending on the age of the victim and other factors. In addition, if a judge finds evidence of deception, violence, threats, abuse of authority, or any other form of intimidation or coercion resulting in sexual intercourse, the minimum sentence increases to six years, regardless of age.

Several prominent cases of child sexual abuse were reported during the year. In September a local journalism forum reported widespread trafficking of disadvantaged Bolivian children. According to the report, international criminal networks lured children across the Argentina-Bolivia border with the promise of well-paying jobs. These networks then sold most of the children for 4,620 pesos ($300) to prostitution rings, exploitative industries, or workshops.

The law prohibits the production and distribution of child pornography, with penalties ranging from six months to four years in prison. While the law does not prohibit the possession of child pornography by individuals for personal use, it provides penalties ranging from four months to two years in prison for possession of child pornography with the intent to distribute it. The law also provides penalties ranging from one month to three years in prison for facilitating access to pornographic shows or materials for minors under the age of 14.

During the year prosecutors from the nationwide "Point of Contact Network against Child Pornography on the Internet" aggressively pursued cases of internet child pornography. From January through September, the Network received 617 reports in Buenos Aires Province and initiated 424 preliminary criminal investigations, 73 of which were unsubstantiated. The remaining cases were under investigation at year's end. The conviction rate was reportedly low due to the difficulty in proving distribution and production. While lengthy judicial processing and bureaucratic inefficiencies occurred, the Network reported national level improvements in the ability to punish offenders.

International Child Abductions: The country is a party to the 1980 Hague Convention on the Civil Aspects of International Child Abduction. See the Department of State's *Annual Report on International Parental Child Abduction* at travel.state.gov/content/childabduction/en/legal/compliance.html.

Anti-Semitism

The Jewish community consists of approximately 250,000 persons. Sporadic acts of anti-Semitic discrimination and vandalism continued. The Delegation of

Argentine Jewish Associations received complaints of anti-Semitism during the year.

The most commonly reported anti-Semitic incidents were slurs posted on various websites, graffiti, verbal slurs, and the desecration of Jewish cemeteries.

On July 5, unidentified individuals threw a plastic bottle filled with cement through the window of the Maccabi Jewish community center in Santa Fe Province. A note attached to the bottle read, "This is a warning, the next one will explode." The note contained the logo of the Islamic State and the Arabic expression "Allahu Akbar (God is great)."

On August 25, students from the Lanus Oeste German School of Buenos Aires engaged in a fistfight with Jewish students from the ORT School of Buenos Aires while both groups were at a nightclub in the resort city of Bariloche. Some of the students from the German school, who deliberately provoked the brawl, wore Hitler mustaches and leather jackets with swastikas painted on them. The director of the German school apologized for the incident, disciplined the school's students, and compelled them to visit the Buenos Aires Holocaust Museum together with the Jewish students.

The investigation continued into the 1994 bombing of the Argentina Israelite Mutual Association (AMIA) community center in Buenos Aires that killed 85 persons. Interpol maintained Red Notices on five Iranians, one Lebanese, and one Colombian suspected in the bombing.

The investigation into the death of Alberto Nisman, the special prosecutor in charge of the AMIA bombing investigation, continued without conclusion as to the motive for his death. In January 2015 Nisman was found dead in his apartment from a gunshot wound to the head. Nisman was scheduled to testify the next day before a congressional committee concerning his allegations that then president Kirchner and associates conspired to convey impunity to the Iranians suspected of planning and executing the AMIA bombing.

Hearings in the AMIA bombing cover-up trial, which accuses government and law enforcement officials and a leader of the country's Jewish community of complicity and false testimony to cover up the 1994 AMIA bombing, continued during the year.

Trafficking in Persons

See the Department of State's *Trafficking in Persons Report* at
www.state.gov/j/tip/rls/tiprpt/.

Persons with Disabilities

The constitution and laws prohibit discrimination against persons with physical,
sensory, intellectual, and mental disabilities in employment, education, air travel
and other transportation, access to health care, the judicial system, or the provision
of other state services. A specific law also mandates access to buildings by
persons with disabilities. According to media reports, the ombudsman of the city
of Buenos Aires reported that only 33 percent of the metropolitan subway stations
had elevators or escalators, and only 29 percent of the stations were equipped with
bathrooms for persons with disabilities.

While the federal government has protective laws, many provinces had not adopted
such laws and had no mechanisms to ensure enforcement. An employment quota
law reserves 4 percent of federal government jobs for persons with disabilities, but
NGOs and advocacy groups claimed the level of disability employment achieved
during the year was less than 1 per cent.

A pattern of inadequate facilities and poor conditions continued in some mental
institutions.

The National Advisory Committee for the Integration of People with Disabilities
under the National Council for Coordination of Social Policies has formal
responsibility for actions to accommodate persons with disabilities.

Indigenous People

The constitution recognizes the ethnic and cultural identities of indigenous people
and states that congress shall protect their right to bilingual education, recognize
their communities and the communal ownership of their ancestral lands, and allow
for their participation in the management of their natural resources. Although there
is no formal process to recognize indigenous tribes or determine who is an
indigenous person, indigenous communities can register with the provincial or
federal government as civic associations.

Indigenous people did not fully participate in the management of their lands or
natural resources, in part because responsibility for implementing the law is

delegated to the 24 provinces, only 11 of which have constitutions recognizing indigenous rights. The NGO International Work Group for Indigenous Affairs reported that implementation of land awards was slow and unpredictable and that bureaucracy, insufficient funding, and opposition by landowners or businesses delayed the process. In 2006 the National Institute for Indigenous Affairs, which awards land rights to indigenous communities and offers indigenous persons constitutional protection and full citizenship rights, began conducting the Territorial Survey Program for Indigenous Communities as part of the land titling process. While the institute initially had four years to conclude the surveying and demarcation, a 2010 law extended the process to 2017.

According to a May 23 press statement of the UN special rapporteur on racism, discrimination, and xenophobia, indigenous people generally lived in extreme poverty, isolation from others, and without access to basic services such as drinkable water, adequate housing, quality health care, employment opportunities, or appropriate and quality education.

Indigenous persons seeking access to justice faced additional unique challenges, including linguistic, cultural, and economic barriers. Most lived in far-flung reaches of the country and must travel considerable distances to access courts. Many provincial courts were unaware of national and international law concerning indigenous peoples' rights to land and natural resources.

Indigenous peoples had lower levels of economic and social development and higher rates of illiteracy than nonindigenous sectors. Poverty rates were higher than average in areas with large indigenous populations. Indigenous people had greater than average rates of illiteracy, chronic disease, and unemployment. Indigenous women faced further discrimination based on gender and reduced economic status. The lack of trained teachers hampered government efforts to offer bilingual education opportunities to indigenous people.

Indigenous peoples continued to lack adequate participation in decisions affecting their ancestral lands. Projects carried out by the agricultural and extractive industries displaced individuals, limited their access to traditional means of livelihood, reduced the area of lands on which they depended, and caused pollution that in some cases endangered the health and welfare of indigenous communities.

Acts of Violence, Discrimination, and Other Abuses Based on Sexual Orientation and Gender Identity

Lesbian, gay, bisexual, transgender, and intersex (LGBTI) persons generally enjoyed the same legal rights and protections as heterosexual persons. No laws criminalize consensual same-sex conduct between adults. LGBTI persons could serve openly in the military.

The law gives transgender persons the right legally to change their gender and name on identity documents without prior approval from a doctor or judge. It also requires public and private health-care plans to cover some parts of hormone therapy and gender reassignment surgery, although the Ministry of Health did not effectively enforce this requirement. In September, Congress enacted legislation prohibiting exclusion of blood donors based upon sexual orientation.

National antidiscrimination laws do not specifically include the terms "sexual orientation or gender identity" as protected grounds, only "sex." There was no official discrimination, however, based on sexual orientation or gender identity in employment, housing, statelessness, or access to education or health care. Overt societal discrimination generally was uncommon, but media and NGOs reported cases of discrimination, violence, and police brutality toward the LGBTI community, especially transgender persons.

HIV and AIDS Social Stigma

There were no known reports of societal violence against persons with HIV/AIDS, but there were occasional reports of discrimination against persons with the disease. According to a private study and survey of stigma and discrimination encountered by persons with HIV/AIDS, 18 percent of those surveyed perceived they had suffered discrimination as a result of their medical condition, primarily from medical providers.

Section 7. Worker Rights

a. Freedom of Association and the Right to Collective Bargaining

The law provides for the rights of workers to form and join independent unions, bargain collectively, and conduct legal strikes; the government generally respected these rights. The law prohibits military and law enforcement personnel from forming and joining unions. In 2015 officers from the Buenos Aires Provincial Police attempted to unionize. The National Labor, Employment, and Social Security Ministry rejected the police petition. The officers appealed the ministry's decision, which remained under consideration in the Supreme Court at year's end.

The government effectively enforced these laws. Complaints of unfair labor practices can be brought before the judiciary. Violations of the law may result in a fine being imposed on the employer or the relevant employers' association, where appropriate. Information regarding fines and other penalties for violations was unavailable. There were few cases of significant delays or appeals in the collective bargaining process.

The law prohibits discrimination against unions and protects workers from dismissal, suspension, and changes in labor conditions. The law requires reinstatement of workers fired for union activity.

The law allows unions to register without prior authorization, and registered trade union organizations may engage in certain activities to represent their members, including petitioning the government and employers. The law grants official trade union status to only one union deemed the "most representative," defined by law as the union that has the highest average proportion of dues-paying members to number of workers represented, per industrial sector within a specific geographical region. Only unions with such official recognition receive trade union immunity from employer reprisals against their officials, are permitted to deduct union dues directly from wages, and may bargain collectively with recourse to conciliation and arbitration. The most representative union bargains on behalf of all workers, and collective agreements cover both union members and nonmembers in the sector. The law requires the Ministry of Labor, Employment, and Social Security to ratify collective bargaining agreements. The International Labor Organization (ILO) requested that the government improve procedures to register trade unions and grant trade union status.

The Argentine Workers Central (CTA) and other labor groups not affiliated with the General Confederation of Labor continued to contend that the legal recognition of only one union per sector conflicted with international standards and prevented these unions from obtaining full legal standing. In 2013 the Supreme Court reaffirmed the need for more than one official union per sector and for amendments to the legislation. Congress had modified the labor law to incorporate the Supreme Court ruling; however, the executive branch granted preliminary recognition to the CTA in 2014. The ILO urged the government to bring the legislation into conformity with international labor standards.

Civil servants and workers in essential services may strike only after a compulsory 15-day conciliation process, and they are subject to the condition that unspecified "minimum services" be rendered. Once the conciliation term expires, civil servants and workers in essential services must give five days' notice to the administrative authority and the public agency where they intend to strike. If "minimum services" were not previously defined in a collective bargaining agreement, all parties then negotiate which minimum services will continue to be provided and a schedule for their provision. The public agency, in turn, must provide clients two days' notice of the impending strike.

Workers exercised freedom of association, and employers respected the right to bargain collectively and to strike.

b. Prohibition of Forced or Compulsory Labor

The law prohibits all forms of forced or compulsory labor, and the government generally enforced such laws. Penalties for violations range from four to 15 years in prison, are comparable to those for other serious offenses, and were sufficiently stringent to deter violations. The Ministry of Justice and Human Rights reported rescuing approximately 304 potential victims of forced labor between January and August 2015. Most of the victims were discovered on agricultural farms and construction sites. The Labor, Employment, and Social Security Ministry carried out several inspections during the year and found various irregularities and potential cases of forced labor. Efforts to hold perpetrators accountable continued during the year, including a criminal case against a construction company in Neuquen Province for trafficking Paraguayans.

Forced labor occurred. Employers subjected a significant number of Bolivians, Paraguayans, and Peruvians, as well as Argentine citizens from poorer northern provinces, to forced labor in the garment sector, agriculture, construction, domestic work, and small businesses (including restaurants and supermarkets). There were reports that Chinese citizens were victims of forced labor in supermarkets. Men, women, and children were victims of forced labor, although victims' typical gender and age varied by employment sector (see section 7.c.).

Also see the Department of State's *Trafficking in Persons Report* at www.state.gov/j/tip/rls/tiprpt/.

c. Prohibition of Child Labor and Minimum Age for Employment

The minimum age for employment is 16. In rare cases labor authorities may authorize a younger child to work as part of a family unit. Children between the ages of 16 and 18 may work in a limited number of job categories and for limited hours if they have completed compulsory schooling, which normally ends at age 18. Children under 18 cannot be hired to perform perilous, arduous, or unhealthy jobs. The law requires employers to provide adequate care for workers' children during work hours to discourage child labor.

Provincial governments and the city government of Buenos Aires are responsible for labor law enforcement. Financial penalties for employing underage workers range from 125 pesos ($8) to 625 pesos ($40) for each child employed. Subsequent violations permit the labor authority to close the company for up to 10 days, and the company is subsequently prohibited from being a government vendor for a year. Prison terms for child labor violations range from one to four years, unless the crime falls under a more serious category. The law excludes parents. These penalties were generally sufficient to deter violations.

While the government generally enforced applicable laws, observers noted some inspectors were acquainted or associated with the persons being inspected, and corruption remained an obstacle to compliance, especially in the provinces.

Child labor occurred. In 2014 the Catholic University of Argentina issued a child labor report (covering the period 2010 to 2013). The report found that 15 percent of children in urban areas between the ages of five and 17 performed some type of work. In rural areas children worked on family and third-party farms producing agricultural goods or raising sheep and pigs. Children working in the agricultural sector often handled pesticides without proper protection. In urban areas some children engaged in domestic service and worked on the street selling goods, shining shoes, and recycling trash. The Labor, Employment, and Social Security Ministry reported a 66 percent decline in child labor rates between 2004 and 2012. According to government sources, some children worked in the manufacturing sector producing such goods as bricks, matches, fireworks, and garments. Children also worked in the mining, fishing, and construction sectors. Officials noted reports of children forced to work as street vendors and beggars in the capital. Commercial sexual exploitation of children occurred as well (see section 6, Children).

Also see the Department of Labor's *Findings on the Worst Forms of Child Labor* at www.dol.gov/ilab/reports/child-labor/findings/.

d. Discrimination with Respect to Employment and Occupation

The law prohibits discrimination with respect to employment or occupation on the basis of race, color, sex, religion, political opinion, national origin or citizenship, social origin, disability, age, language, and HIV-positive status or other communicable disease.

The government enforced these laws more effectively in cases where employees were terminated because of discrimination, but there were no statistics available on how the law was applied in cases of discrimination during the hiring of employees.

The most prevalent cases of workplace discrimination were based on gender (see section 6, Women) and age. Discrimination also occurred on the basis of HIV-positive status (see section 6, HIV/AIDS and Social Stigma) and against individuals of indigenous origin. In April the Labor, Employment, and Social Security Ministry issued a resolution promoting progressive actions in the workplace and prohibited companies from blood screening for HIV when conducting employment-related medical screening.

e. Acceptable Conditions of Work

In September the government increased the monthly minimum wage for workers to 7,560 pesos ($490). According to the latest available official data from the National Census and Statistics Institute, issued in September, a family of four needed 12,489 pesos ($810) to remain above the poverty line.

Federal law sets standards in the areas of hours and occupational safety and health. The maximum workday is eight hours, and the maximum workweek is 48 hours. Overtime pay is required for hours worked in excess of these limits. The law prohibits excessive overtime and defines permissible levels of overtime as three hours a day. The law sets minimums for periods of rest, requiring a minimum of 12 hours of rest prior to the start of a new workday. Sundays are holidays, and those required to work on Sundays are paid double. Labor law mandates between 14 and 35 days of paid vacation, depending on the length of the worker's service.

The law sets premium pay for overtime, adding an extra 50 percent of the hourly rate on ordinary days and 100 percent on Saturday afternoons, Sundays, and holidays. Employees cannot be forced to work overtime unless work stoppage would risk or cause injury, the need for overtime is caused by an act of God, or other exceptional reasons affecting the national economy or "unusual and unpredictable situations" affecting businesses occur.

The government sets occupational safety and health standards, which were current and appropriate for the main industries in the country. The law requires employers to insure their employees against accidents at the workplace and when traveling to and from work. The law requires employers either to provide insurance through a labor-risk insurance entity or to provide their own insurance to employees to meet requirements specified by the national insurance regulator. In 2012 Congress amended the Labor Risks Law to increase compensation for a worker's death or incapacitation, while limiting the worker's right to file a complaint if he or she accepts the insurance company's compensation.

Laws governing acceptable conditions of work were not enforced universally, particularly for workers in the informal sector. The Labor, Employment, and Social Security Ministry has responsibility for enforcing legislation related to working conditions. The ministry continued inspections to ensure companies registered their workers are registered and formally employed. During the year the ministry reported that it had 400 labor inspectors. The ministry conducted inspections in various provinces during the year. Statistics on the number of inspections during the year, violations encountered by inspectors, and fines or penalties imposed were not publicly available. According to senior officials in the labor ministry, approximately three to four million citizens were engaged in the informal sector. The Superintendency of Labor Risk served as the enforcement agency to monitor compliance with health and safety laws and the activities of the labor risk insurance companies.

Most workers in the formal sector earned significantly more than the minimum wage. The minimum wage generally served to mark the minimum pay an informal worker should receive, although formal workers' pay was usually higher.

The Superintendency of Labor Risk statistics for 2015 indicated there were, on average, 46.4 worker fatalities per million workers. Workers could not always recuse themselves from situations that endangered their health or safety without jeopardy to their employment, and authorities did not effectively protect employees in these circumstances.